amazing baby™

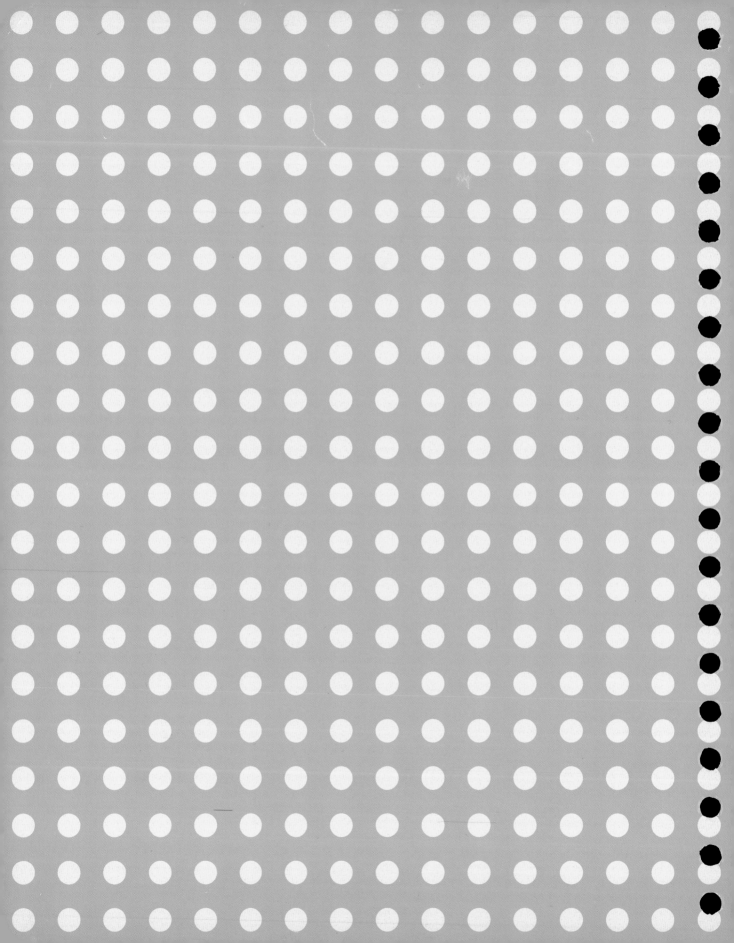

amazing baby™

a first guide to

baby
signing

Silver Dolphin
San Diego, California

Silver Dolphin Books

An imprint of the Advantage Publishers Group
10350 Barnes Canyon Road, San Diego, CA 92121
www.silverdolphinbooks.com

First edition published in the UK in 2005 by Templar Publishing.
This edition published by Silver Dolphin Books.
Text © 2007 by Katie Mayne, TinyTalk
Design and illustration © 2007 by The Templar Company plc

amazing baby™ is an imprint of The Templar Company plc

ISBN-13: 978-1-59223-525-4
ISBN-10: 1-59223-525-5

Graphics by Emma Dodd
Photography by Andrew Coombes
With thanks to all the TinyTalk babies
and moms who took part in this project

Printed in China

1 2 3 4 5 11 10 09 08 07

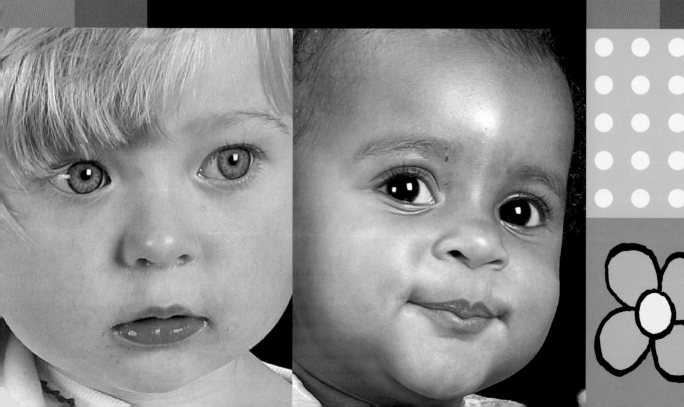

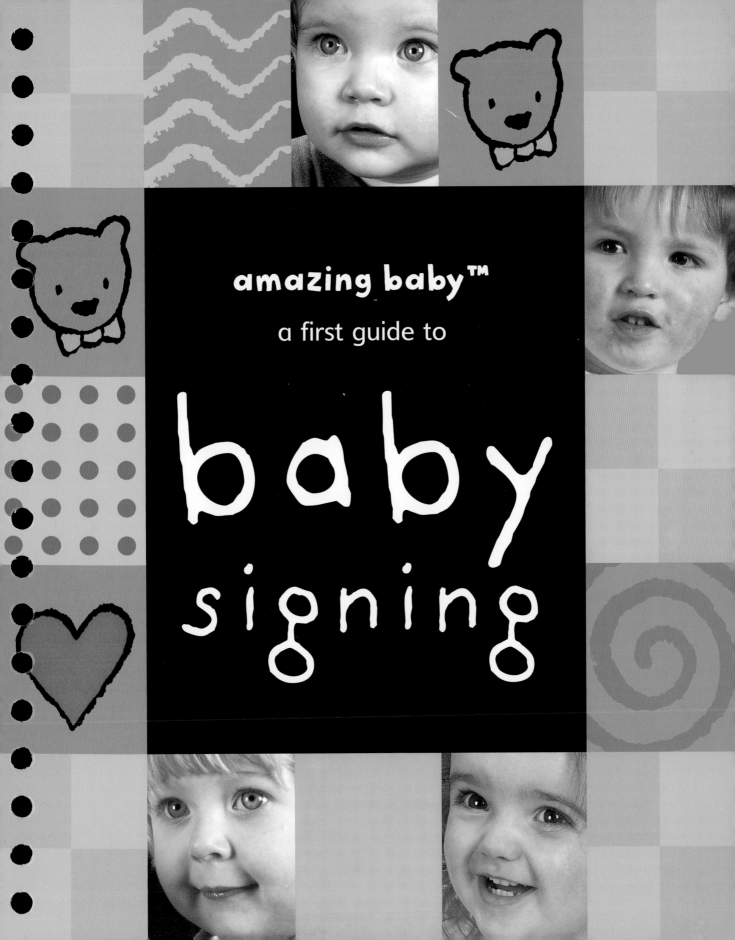

amazing baby™

a first guide to

baby signing

amazing baby™

Language helps us to
make sense of our world.
Babies understand so much
before they can talk. Using signs
encourages early word play,
language development,
and comprehension.
Babies who understand and are
understood are happy babies!

Katie Mayne, author

why? and how?

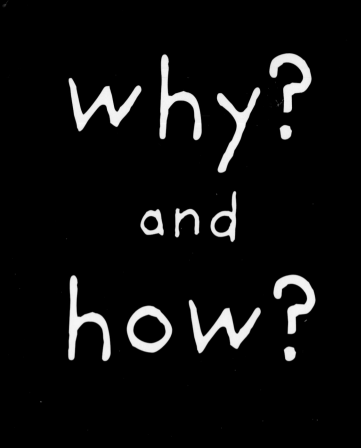

why?

Sign language provides a way for babies to tell others what they want or what they are thinking about. It also helps them understand what is being said to them. When they are around six to nine months old, babies realize that objects have names (i.e., they grasp the concept of vocabulary). They also have good control of their hands. Babies develop this hand control long before they develop enough control over, and coordination of, their vocal cords, lips, tongue, and teeth to make recognizable words. Baby sign language bridges this gap.

how?

Visual clues (i.e., signs) help babies make sense of the words that they hear as they look at things around them. Every time an object is introduced, the object's name is both said and signed. Only one or two signs, such as "milk" and "food," are introduced at first. Babies can repeat the sign back to you with understanding as soon as four to six weeks later. Other signs can then be introduced, a few at a time. These will be learned much more quickly and a wide vocabulary will develop.

the signs

starter signs

1 milk
2 food/eat
3 drink
4 more & all gone!

instructional signs

5 look & see
6 sit
7 please & thank you
8 where?
9 what?
10 who?

family signs

11 mommy & daddy
12 baby & hug

clothing signs

13 coat & hat
14 socks
15 shoes

indoor signs

16 toy/play
17 phone
18 house/home

mealtime signs

19 apple

20 banana

21 cookie

22 teeth

23 spoon

evening signs

24 bath & water

25 book

26 bed/sleep

outdoor signs

27 car   31 flower

28 park   32 plane

29 boat   33 sun

30 tree   34 rain

animal signs

35 bird

36 cat

37 dog

38 fish

39 duck

advanced signs

40 diaper

41 toilet

42 pain

43 clean & dirty

44 hot & cold

what we will do!

starter signs

Starter signs are the first ones to introduce to your baby. They relate to basic needs, such as thirst and hunger, and therefore will be straightforward for you to teach and easy for your baby to learn and use.

instructional signs

We will guide you through the signs step by step. The signs chosen relate to the most common objects in a young child's environment. They are also linked to the first speech sounds and words spoken. The signs are grouped into sections for ease of reference.

Instructional signs are mainly for your use, to extend your communication, rather than simply using a string of nouns and adjectives. With these items of vocabulary you can ask questions such as "What's this?" or make statements such as "Look at these flowers!"

family signs

You can add to this collection by creating "sign names." This is when you say the person's name, such as "Grandma," as you sign a visual characteristic of theirs, such as "curly hair." This becomes their personal sign name.

clothing signs & indoor signs

These two sections show you signs for everyday items around the house.

mealtime signs

Mealtimes are an opportunity to introduce new signs, as your baby will be attentive to words and their signs, in particular those relating to food. This section also includes signs for words such as "spoon" and "teeth."

evening signs

Evening signs aid the bedtime routine and help children gain a sense of preparation for the sequence of events.

outdoor signs

Outdoor signs include signs for weather—e.g., "sun" or "rain."

animal signs

Animal signs include "duck," one of the first signs that babies master, as it is easily understood—and ducks are seen everywhere!

advanced signs

The last section gives examples of some advanced signs relating to slightly later stages of development, such as toilet training, or advanced concepts such as adjectives—e.g., "hot" and "cold."

get ready...

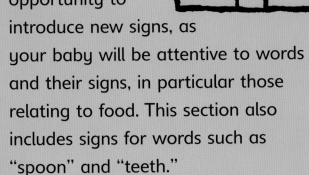

how you will do it!

Start with a couple of signs, such as "milk" and "food." Make sure that your baby is facing you and can clearly see and focus on your face, particularly your mouth and your hands. Many people start teaching their signs at mealtimes, when their baby is hungry and motivated.

Try to keep background noise to a minimum if you can. As you sign, use plenty of facial expression, body language, and variety in the pitch and intonation of your voice. Don't be surprised if your baby finds this amusing and laughs at you! Repeat the sign every time you say the word, always showing the object, too.

Try to have each object on hand as it is introduced, such as milk, food, or a book. You could also point to pictures in a book. Begin your signing when you know that your child will be most responsive.

Many signs require both hands but some need only one. If you are right-handed, use your right hand, and vice versa if you are left-handed.

After you have introduced the signs a few times, you can begin to mold your child's hand gently into the hand shapes. Make up games and rhymes, sing songs, or use puppets to reinforce the language. Always keep it relaxed and fun. If your child is not in the mood to learn, leave it until another time.

Other members of the family, including siblings, should learn and use the signs too. All related adults, especially those who provide child care, need to be able to use and recognize the signs.

When your baby shows an understanding of the first concepts and signs, it won't be long until they are using the signs to you.

Once they realize that they can give you a message by using a sign (this can be as soon as four to six weeks after the signs have been introduced), they will be thrilled! What a great game! You need to think about your response to potentially constant requests for food. (Try slices of banana or single raisins.)

Your baby's first signs may be a little inaccurate and require gentle correction. Be sure to show that you are pleased with their attempts. Show them the correct sign in your response, such as, "Yes, that's right—it is a book!" while repeating the sign. The correct signs will be learned in time.

Other signs can then be slowly introduced, a few at a time, and the signs should be relevant to your home environment.

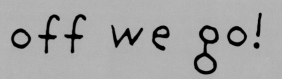

off we go!

starter signs

1 milk
2 food/eat
3 drink
4 more & all gone!

milk

breast-feed

step 1

Hold your hand open, across and against your chest as if it is a mouth at the breast.

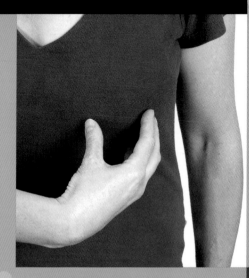

step 2

Bring your thumb and fingertips together as you move your hand away from your chest.

step 3

Return your hand to the open position and repeat step 2.

milk
(squeezing an udder!)

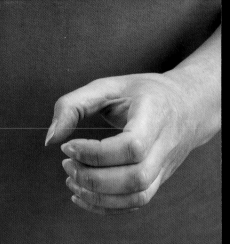

step 1
Hold your hand upright as if holding a bottle.

step 2
Bring your fingers and thumb in to make a fist shape. Open your hand again and repeat.

19

food/eat

step 1

Press the tips of your fingers and thumb together. Start to say the word "food."

step 2

Move your hand toward your mouth and touch your lips.

step 3

Pull away from your mouth as you finish saying "food." Keep your hand in the same position throughout. Repeat for "eat."

clever boy!

21

drink

step 1
Hold your hand in front of you, with fingers and thumb curled as if holding a cup.

step 2
Raise your hand to your mouth as if drinking.

step 3
Lower the hand to the original position.

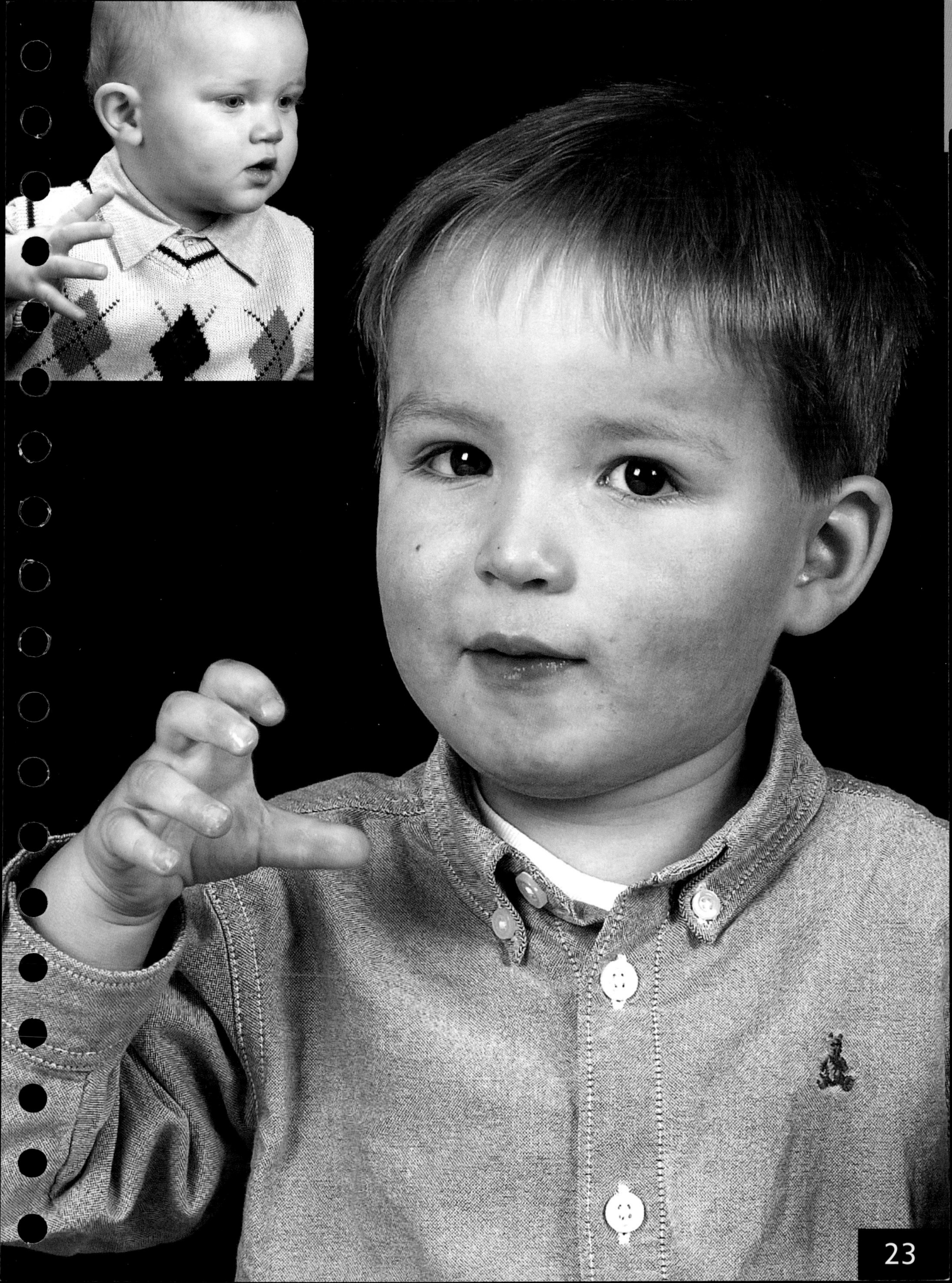

4

more

step 1
Hold your hands in front of you, palms facing inward, with the thumb touching the fingertips on each hand.

step 2
Bring your hands together, so the tips of your fingers touch. Then repeat.

24

all gone!

step 1
Hold your hands up, with your palms facing inward.

step 2
Twist both hands so the palms face outward.

25

instructional signs

look

step 1

With your first two fingers in a "V," hold your hand to your face, with your palm facing inward and your index fingertip below your eye.

step 2

Move your hand forward and away from your face, pointing your fingers toward the object you are looking at.

see

step 1

Point your index finger and hold your hand to the side of your face, with your palm facing inward and your index fingertip below your eye.

step 2

Move your hand forward and away from your face, pointing your finger toward the object you are seeing.

sit

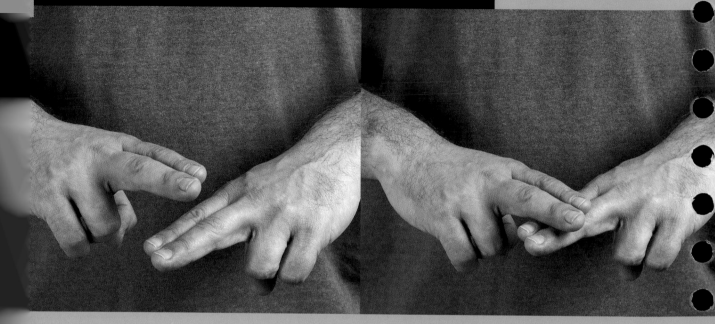

step 1
Place the first two fingers of one hand above the first two fingers of the other hand, palms down.

step 2
Tap your fingers together as you say "sit."

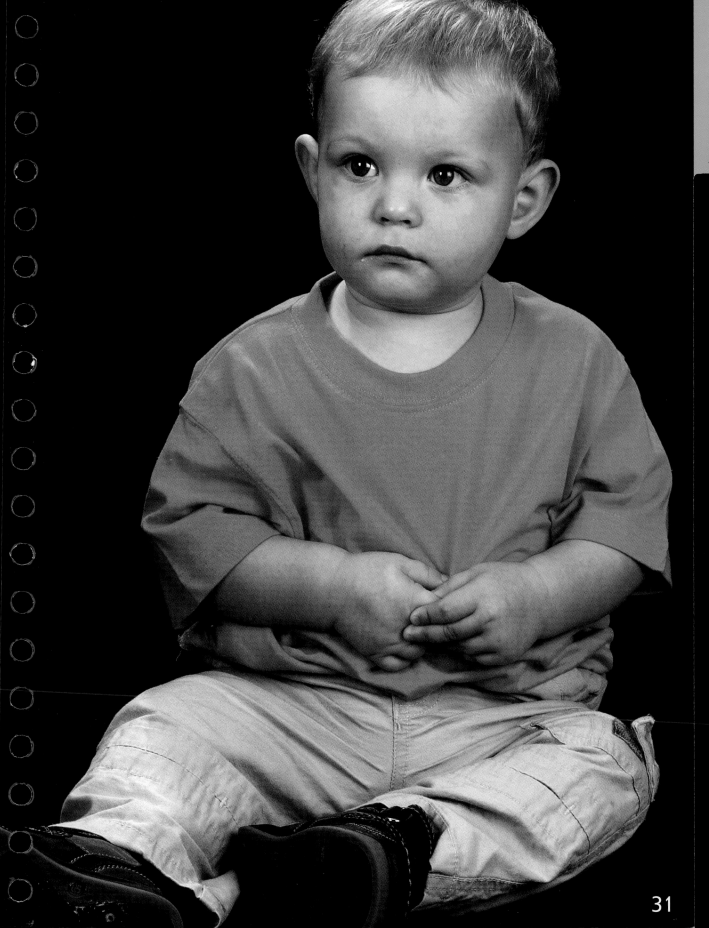

please

step 1

As you say "please," put your open hand over the center of your chest, then move it in a clockwise circular motion a few times.

thank you

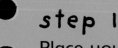

step 1
Place your fingers flat against your chin.

step 2
As you say "thank you," move your hand forward.

where?

step 1
Point your index finger up, palm away.

step 2
Wave your finger from side to side, in short movements.

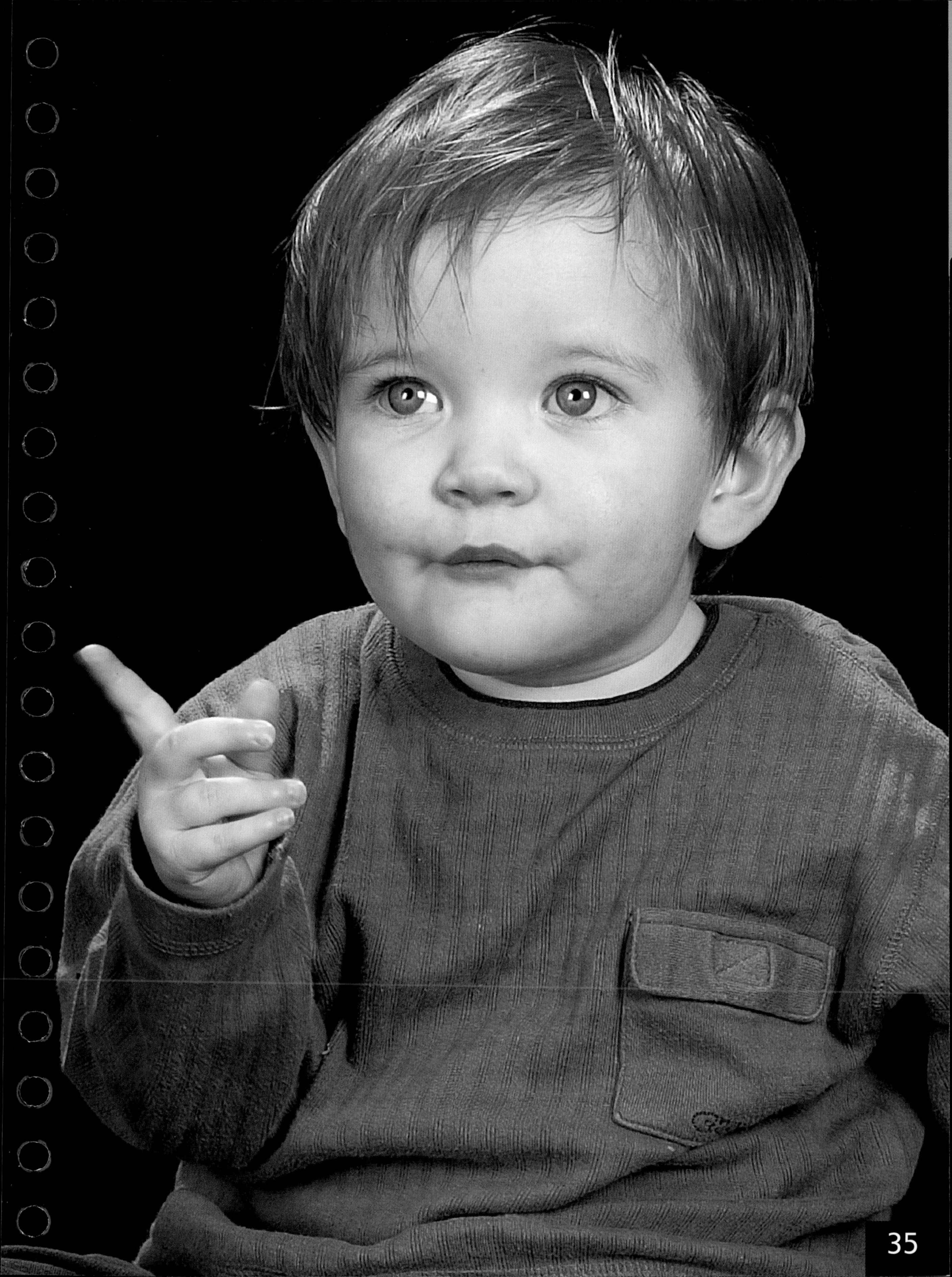

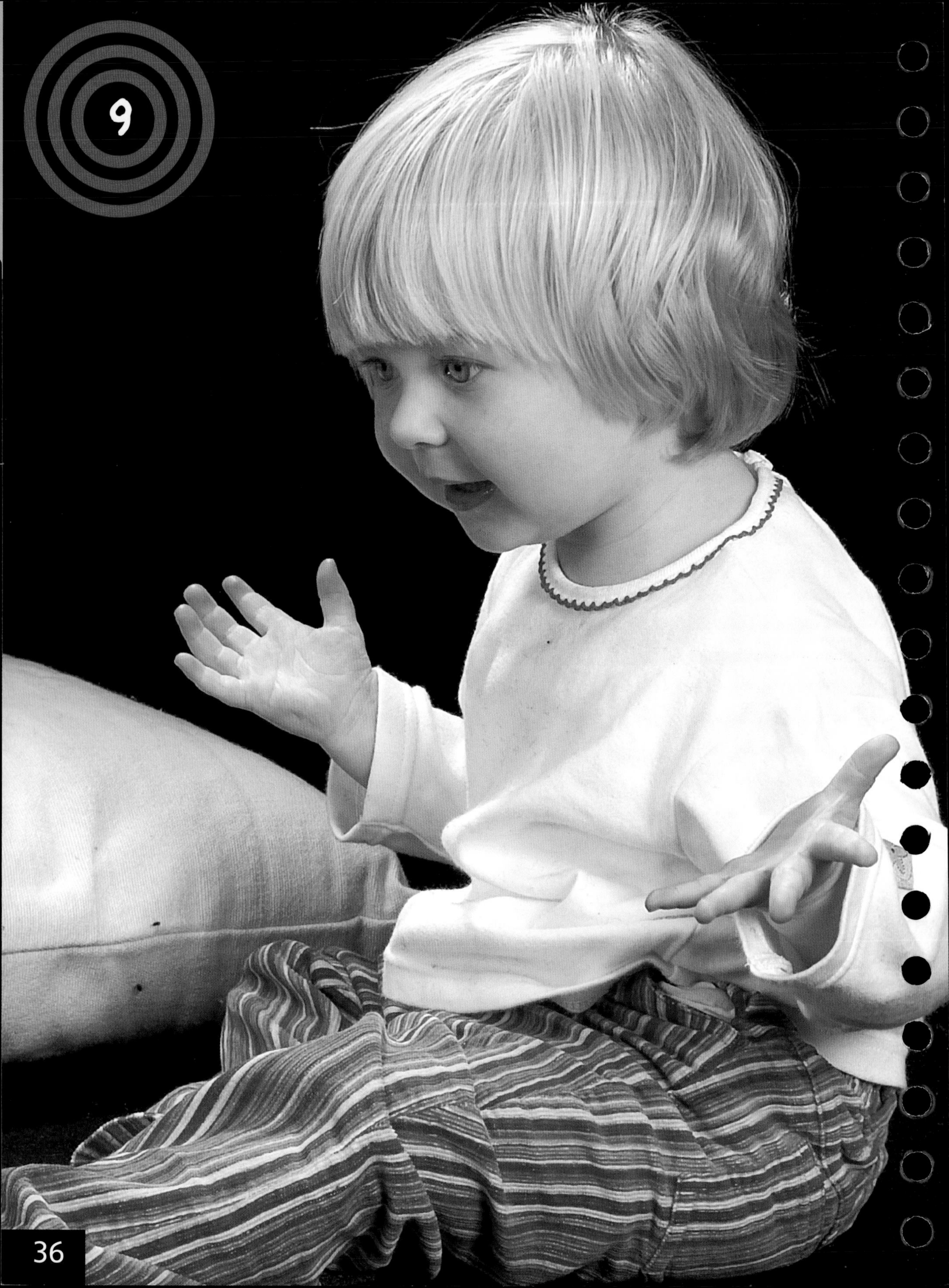

what?

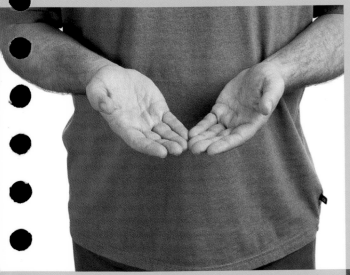

step 1
Hold your hands out, palms up, with little fingertips touching.

step 2
Move your palms apart and out to the sides in a circular motion.

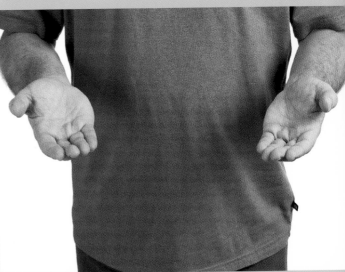

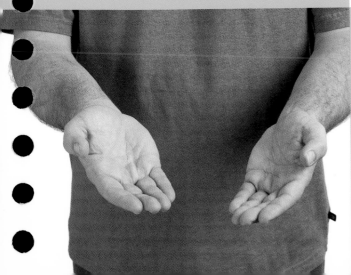

step 3
Continue in a circular motion, moving your palms back to their starting positions. Repeat.

10

who?

step 1
Point your index finger upward, palm toward you.

step 2
Rotate your finger in small circles (toward you, then away).

family signs

step 1
Place the thumb of one hand against your chin, with your fingers open.

step 2
Tap several times as you say "mommy."

daddy

step 1

Place the thumb of
one hand against
your forehead, with
your fingers open.

step 2

Tap several times as
you say "daddy."

baby

step 1

"Cradle" your hands together, one hand laid upon the other.

hug

step 1
Extend your arms in front of your body with your palms facing inward.

step 2
Pull your arms in toward your body while crossing them.

step 3
Wrap your crossed arms around yourself, as if hugging.

45

clothing signs

 **13**

coat

step 1
Clench both hands. Hold them up by your shoulders, palms facing away from the body.

step 2
Bring your hands down toward your chest as if pulling on a coat.

step 3
Bring your fists together in front of your chest.

hat

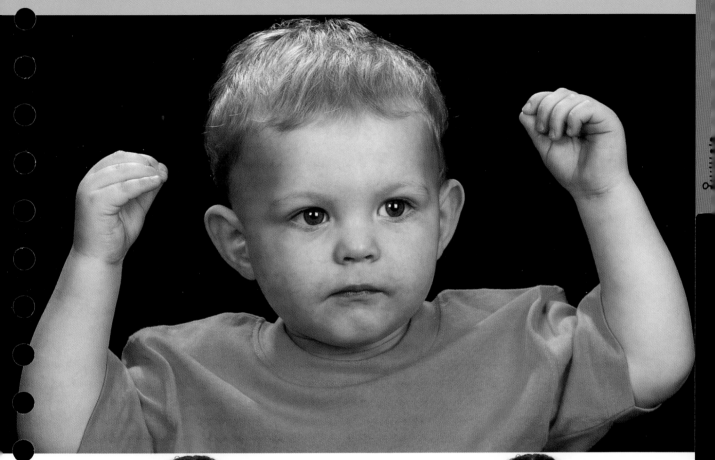

step 1
Clench your hands into fists and hold them up on either side of your head.

step 2
Pull your clenched hands down past your ears, as if pulling on a hat.

49

socks

step 1
Hold your hands at waist level, slightly to your left. Point your index fingers and thumbs downward, keeping them apart.

step 2
Pinch the index finger and the thumb of each hand together as you move your hands upward, as if pulling up a sock.

step 3
Hold your hands at waist level, slightly to your right this time. Point index fingers and thumbs downward, keeping them apart.

step 4
Pinch the index finger and the thumb of each hand together as you move your hands upward.

shoes

step 1
Make two fists, palms facing downward.

step 2
Tap your fists together.

step 3

Repeat steps
1 and 2, tapping
your fists together
once more.

indoor signs

16

toy/
play

step 1
Hold your hands in front of you with your thumbs and little fingers extended.

step 2
Turn your wrists from side to side, keeping your thumb and little finger extended.

phone

ring, ring!

step 1
Curl the middle three fingers of your hand under. Extend your thumb and little finger. Your thumb should be touching your ear.

house/ home

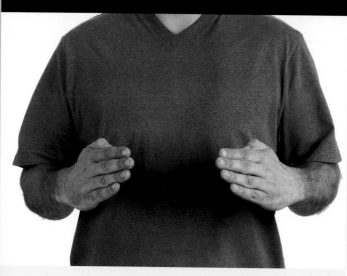

step 1

With fingers on both hands straight and thumbs tightly pressed against your index fingers, touch the fingertips of both hands together.

indoor

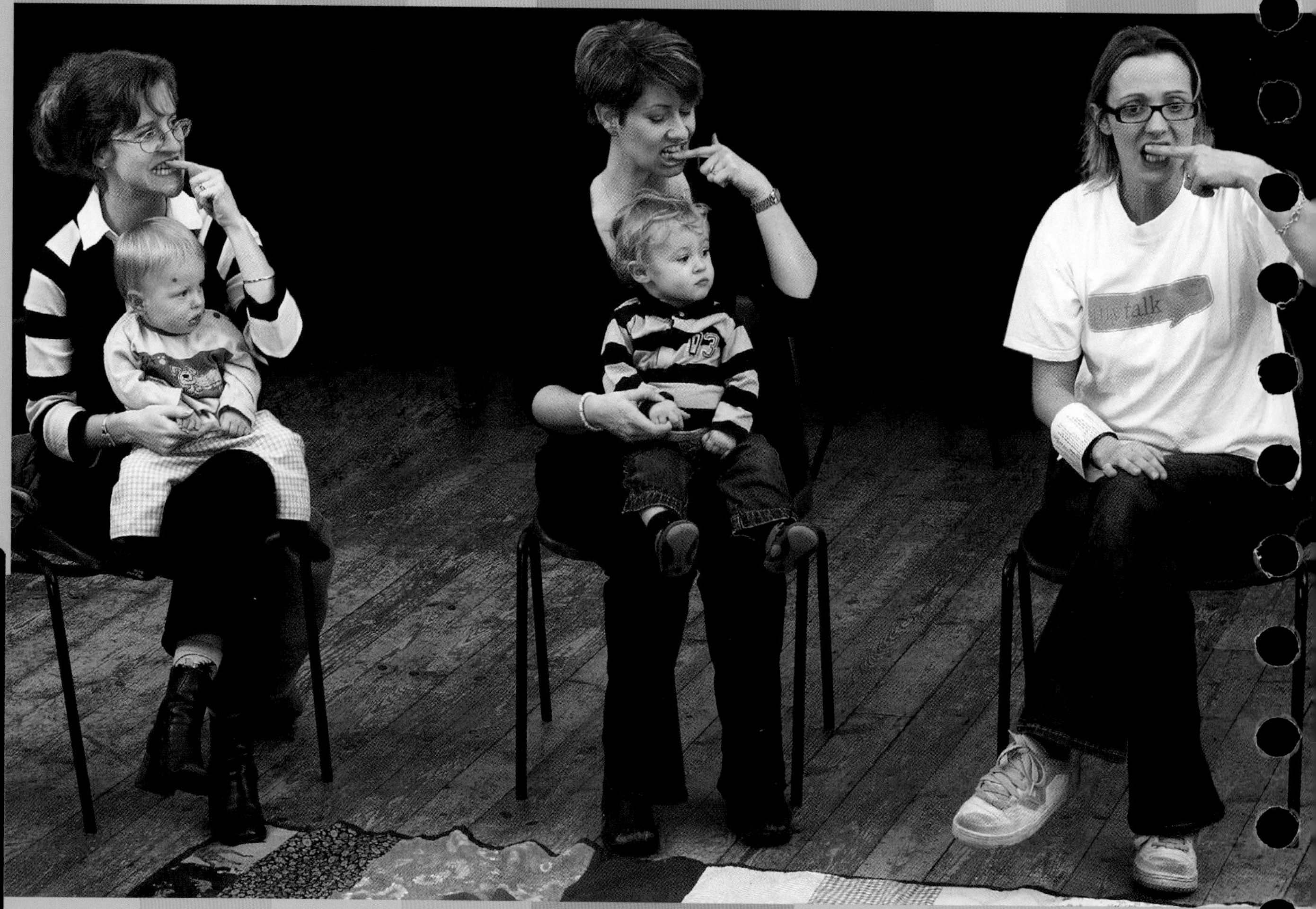

mealtime signs

19 apple

20 banana

21 cookie

22 teeth

23 spoon

apple

step 1
Curve your hand into a "C" shape and hold at your mouth, palm facing you.

step 2
Turn your wrist out and away from you as if you are taking a bite.

64

⟨20⟩ banana

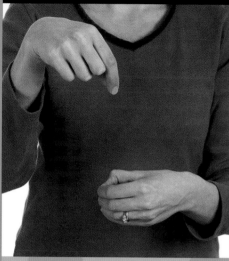

step 1

With one hand cupped, mime holding a banana. With your other hand, pinch your thumb and index finger and mime peeling the banana, starting at the top.

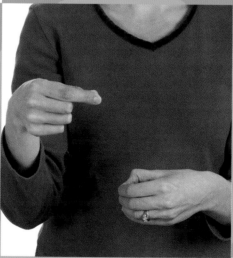

step 2

Keeping your thumb and index finger pinched, "peel" the banana . . .

step 3

. . . to the bottom! Repeat the peeling motion several times around the sides of the banana.

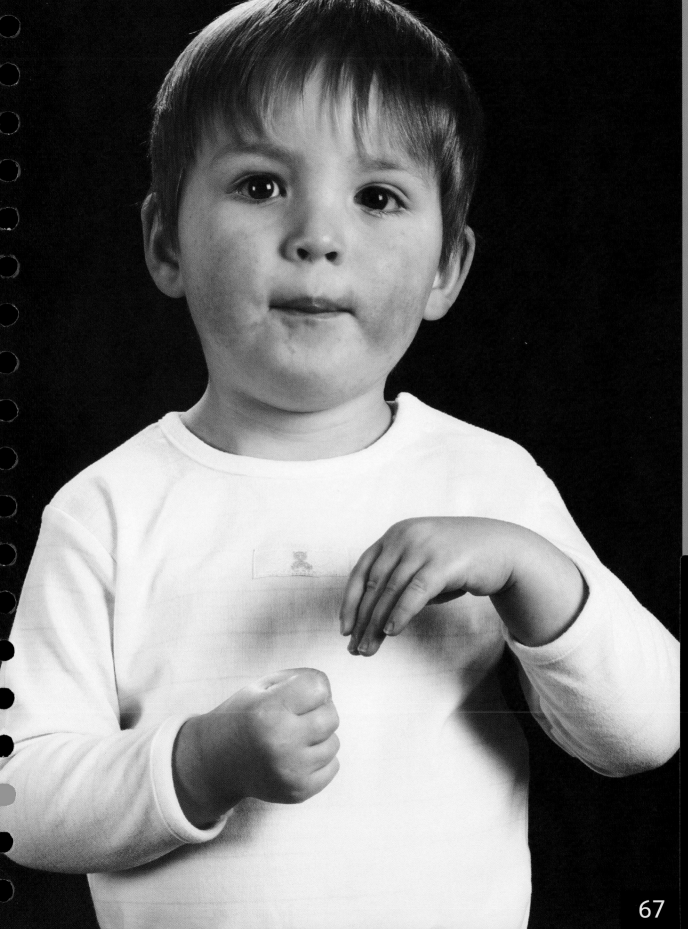

21 cookie

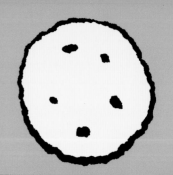

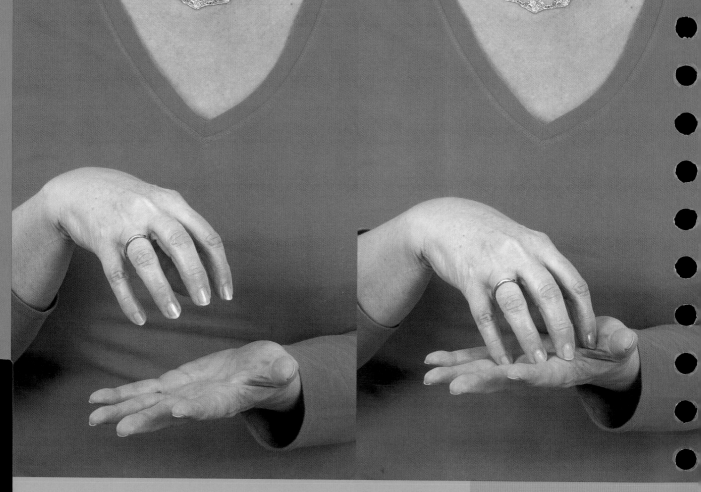

step 1

Hold one hand in front of you with your palm open. Cup the other hand above your open palm.

step 2

Touch the open palm with your cupped hand, as if you are cutting out cookies from cookie dough!

teeth

step 1

Simple—with your mouth open and teeth showing, point to your teeth. This is an example to show how easily you can sign many other parts of the body.

spoon

mealtime

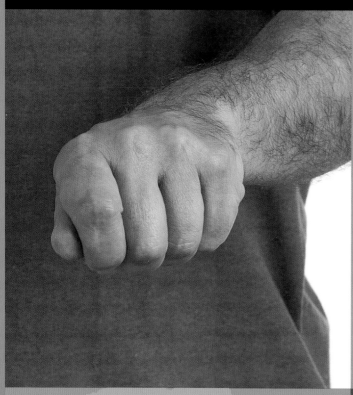

step 1
Clench your fist with your thumb resting against the crook of your bent index finger, as if clasping a spoon, palm down.

step 2
Twist your wrist as if scooping with the spoon, so that your thumbnail now faces upward.

evening signs

24 bath & water
25 book
26 bed/sleep

bath

step 1
Make both hands into fists. Hold as if gripping a towel.

step 2
Wave your forearms to one side, miming a drying action.

step 3
Wave your forearms to the other side. Repeat steps 2 and 3.

water

step 1

With your palm open, tap your index finger against your chin.

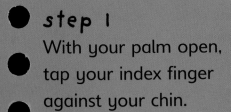

step 2

Repeat this movement while saying "water."

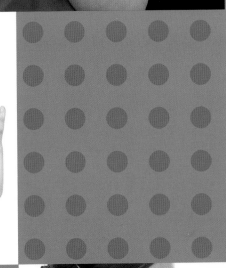

77

book

step 1
Hold your hands together, palms touching (like a closed book) with fingers pointing away from you and thumbnails facing up.

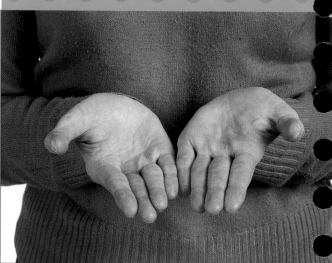

step 2
Open up your hands as if opening a book.

bed/ sleep

step 1

With hands together, palms touching, tilt your head against your hands. For "sleep," close your eyes as if sleeping.

outdoor signs

27 car

28 park

29 boat

30 tree

31 flower

32 plane

33 sun

34 rain

car

vroom, vroom!

off we go!

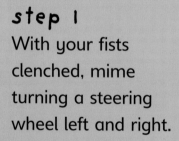

step 1
With your fists clenched, mime turning a steering wheel left and right.

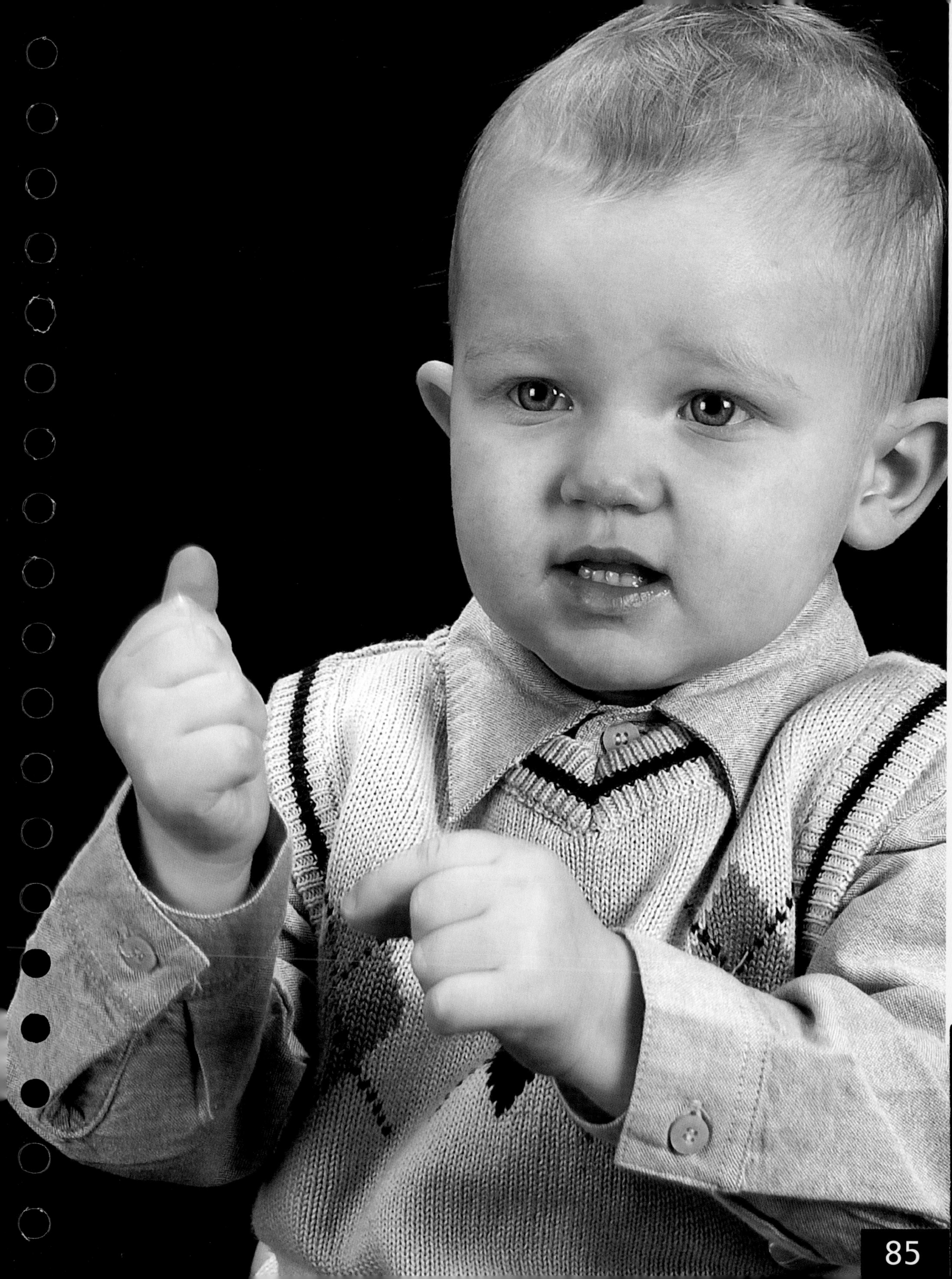

28

park

step 1

Hold your arm out to the side, palm down, keeping your fingers and thumb together.

step 2

Move your arm across your body in an arc, keeping your palm down, as if sweeping across an open space.

step 3

Place your hand against your other arm, palm down.

outdoor

87

boat

step 1

Make your hands into a "boat" shape—palms facing each other, fingertips touching and pointing away from you.

step 2

Move your hands forward with fingertips still touching.

30

tree

outdoor

90

step 1

Bend one arm at the elbow, hand raised, palm facing away, and fingers apart. Place the other arm across your body. Its hand should be flat with palm down, and placed under your other elbow.

step 2

Move your raised arm from side to side, to show a tree blowing in the breeze.

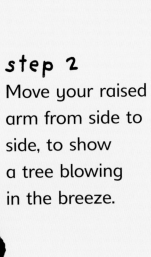

flower

step 1
Pinch together the index finger and thumb of one hand.

step 2
Raise your fingers to one nostril and mime sniffing a flower.

step 3
Repeat at the other nostril.

plane

step 1

Curl the middle three fingers of one hand under and extend your thumb and little finger. With your elbow crooked slightly, hold your arm out so your knuckles are facing away from your body.

step 2

Move your arm up and across your body diagonally, toward your other shoulder.

step 3

Keep moving your arm upward until your hand is up to the height of your shoulder.

outdoor

sun

step 1
Bend one arm at the elbow, hand raised in a fist, higher than your head, palm facing you.

step 2
Open your fingers out, palm down.

light rain

34

step 1
Raise both hands in front of you, palms down and fingers apart.

step 2
Gently bring both arms down together . . .

step 3
. . . wriggling your fingers as you do so.

step 1
Hold both hands raised at shoulder height and at a slight angle.

step 2
Forcefully bring both arms down together . . .

step 3
. . . in a series of stages.

outdoor

animal signs

35 bird

36 cat

37 dog

38 fish

39 duck

bird

step 1
Hold the thumb and index finger of one hand by your mouth, as a beak.

step 2
Pinch your thumb and finger together to mime the bird's beak closing. Repeat.

cat

step 1

Hold your hands to your face, palms facing you and fingertips pointing toward your nose.

step 2

Move your hands apart across your face, while curling your fingers and thumbs, miming whiskers!

animal

dog

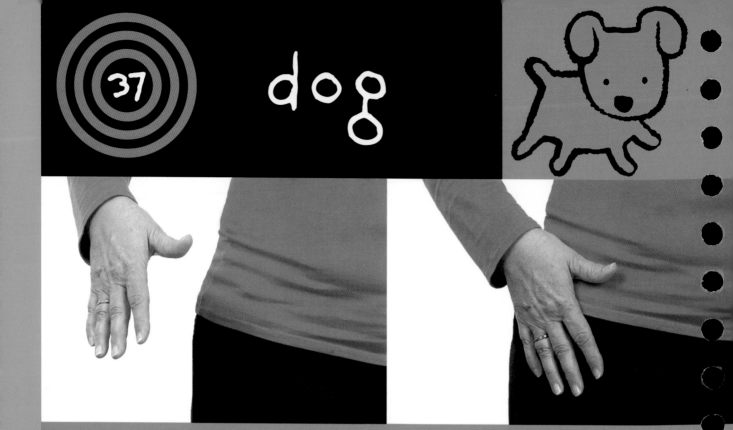

step 1

Pat your thigh with the palm of your hand, as if you are calling a dog.

animal

fish

step 1
Bend one arm at the elbow at waist level. Your hand should be flat, fingers and thumb together, thumbnail facing up.

step 2
Move your arm across your body, turning your hand inward to indicate a fish swimming.

step 3
Move your arm further across your body, turning your hand slightly outward this time.

step 4
Repeat hand movements as the "fish" keeps swimming!

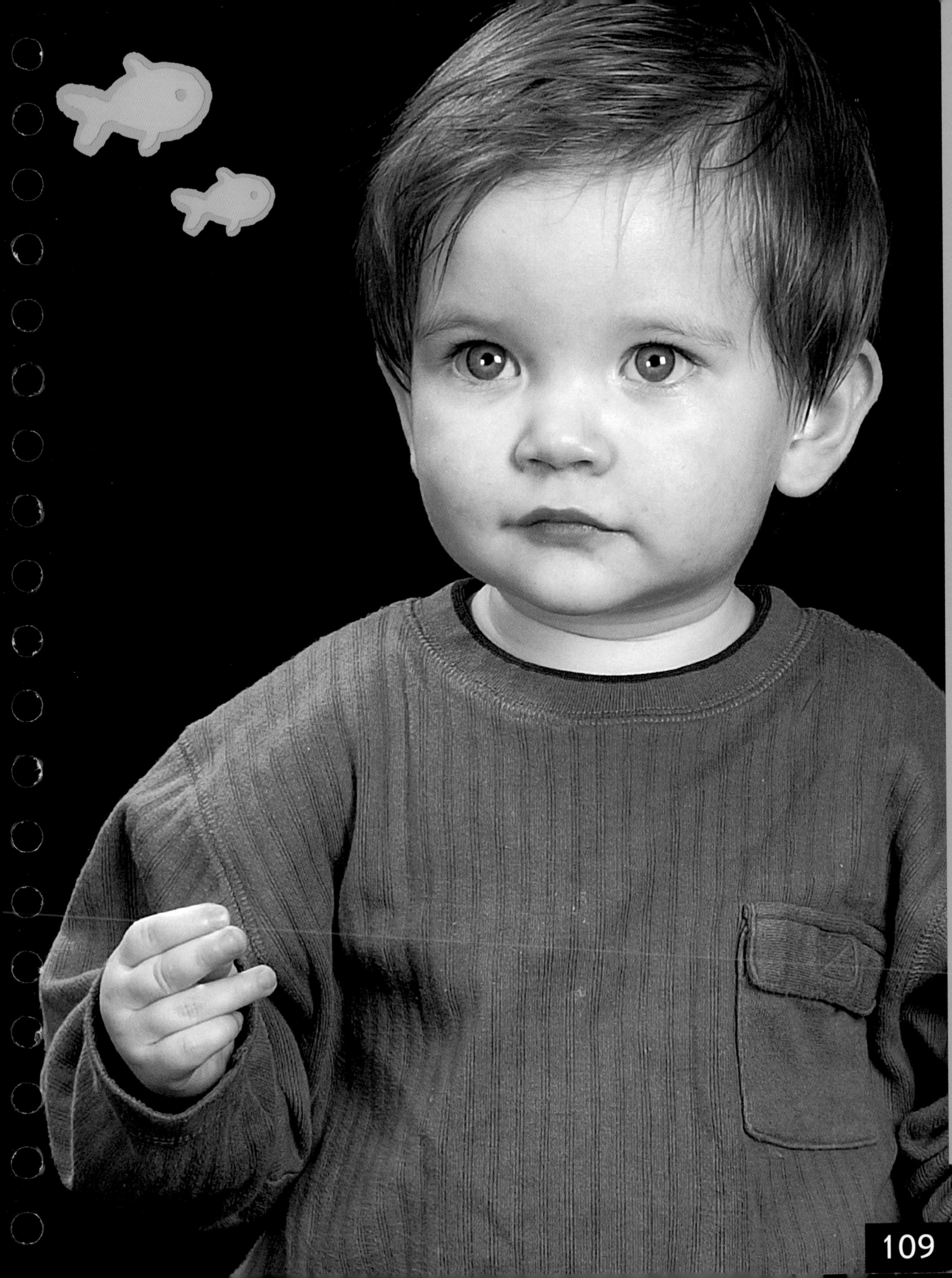

animal

duck

step 1
Hold the fingers and thumb of one hand by your mouth, as a beak.

step 2
Pinch your fingers and thumb to mime the duck's beak closing. Repeat.

animal

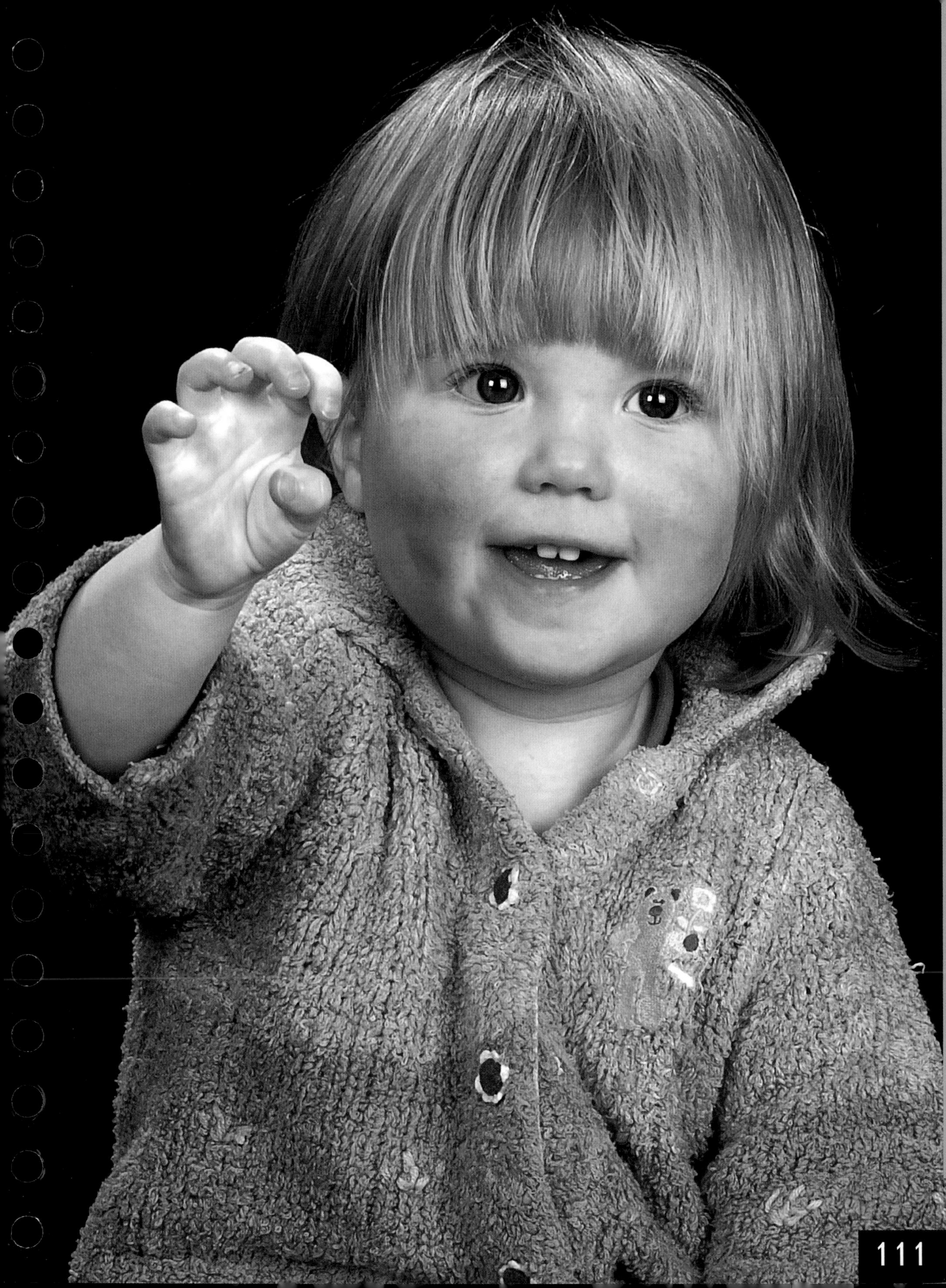

advanced signs

40 diaper

41 toilet

42 pain

43 clean & dirty

44 hot & cold

40

diaper

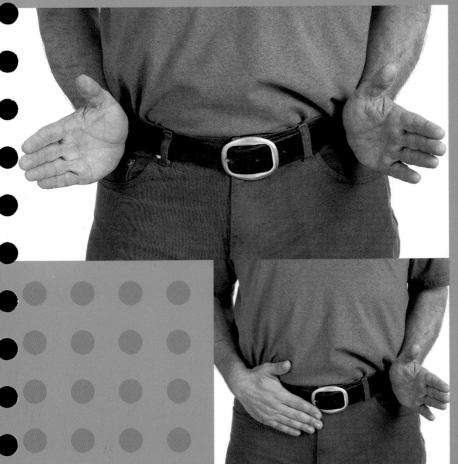

step 1
Put your hands at your waist, with your wrists touching your hips and fingers pointing outward.

step 2
Move one hand in and place it flat on your waist, as if sealing a fastener.

step 3
Repeat with the other hand.

toilet

step 1
Hold your fist at shoulder height and shake your wrist quickly from side to side.

pain

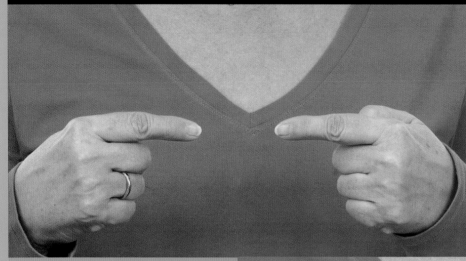

step 1
Extend your index fingers and hold your hands up with your palms facing in.

step 2
Tap the tips of your fingers together several times.

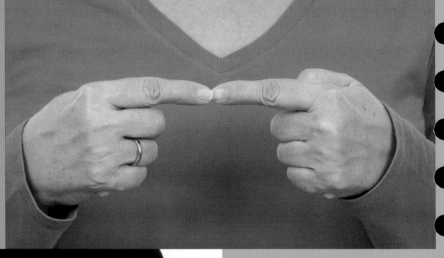

step 3
Sign at the parts of the body that are in pain—e.g., the head, teeth, or tummy.

head!

teeth!

tummy!

knee!

clean

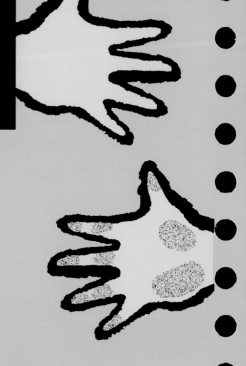

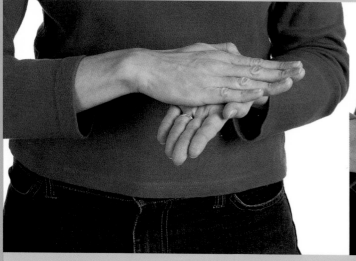
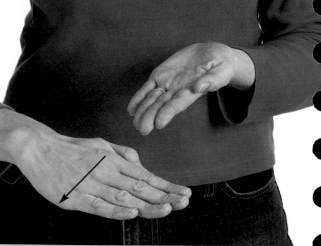

step 1
Hold one hand out flat, palm facing upward. Place your other hand on top, palm down, fingers pointing in a different direction.

step 2
Slowly sweep the top hand along the bottom hand, away from you.

dirty

step 1
Wiggle the fingers of one hand under your chin, with your palm down.

121

hot

hot drink or food

step 1
Cup your hand over your mouth.

step 2
Twist your wrist quickly away from your mouth . . .

step 3
. . . and open up your hand (as if spitting out some hot food!).

hot day

step 1
Put your hand in front of your forehead, palm facing you.

step 2
Draw your hand across your forehead . . .

step 3
. . . while closing your fingers.

cold

step 1
Hold your arms at your sides, elbows bent, with your fists clenched and palms facing each other.

step 2
Bring your elbows in closer to your waist.

step 3
Shake your arms and fists as if shivering.

advanced

Baby signs fall away naturally when children realize that they are understood through their spoken words alone (and that they can use their hands to do other things). However, baby signing continues to be of value. When toddlers are tired or frustrated, signs are often used to reinforce the message that they are trying to communicate. They can also have lots of fun and feel very important introducing and teaching baby sign language to any new little brother or sister.

Have lots of fun with baby signing!

index

hat	49	see	29
home	60	shoes	52
hot	122	sit	30
house	60	sleep	80
hug	45	socks	50
look	28	spoon	72
milk	18	sun	96
mommy	42	teeth	70
more	24	thank you	33
pain	118	toilet	116
park	86	toy	56
phone	58	tree	90
plane	94	water	77
play	56	what?	36
please	32	where?	34
rain (heavy)	99	who?	38
rain (light)	98